Living with Confidence in a Chaotic World

Participant's Guide

Living with Confidence in a Chaotic World

Discovering What on Earth We Should Do Now

DVD-Based Study
Participant's Guide

David Jeremiah

THOMAS NELSON
Since 1798

NASHVILLE   DALLAS   MEXICO CITY   RIO DE JANEIRO   BEIJING

Published by Thomas Nelson, Inc., PO Box 141000, Nashville, Tennessee, 37214.

Published in association with Yates & Yates, LLP, Attorneys and Counselors, Orange, California.

Typesetting by Gregory C. Benoit Publishing, Old Mystic, CT GCB

ISBN-9781418542917

Printed in the United States of America

4 5 6 13 12 11 10 09

Contents

Introductory Session

This is an 11-week series based on Dr. David Jeremiah's book *Living with Confidence in a Chaotic World: What on Earth Should We Do Now?*, a follow-up to his bestselling book, *What in the World Is Going On?* Each video is 10–20 minutes, to be followed by the discussion facilitated in this book.

This first session is a recap of all the recent world events covered in *What in the World Is Going On?*, and the remainder of the study is dedicated to discovering what on earth we should do in response.

OPEN IN PRAYER

DISCUSS TOGETHER

Introductions

Everyone should participate in this exercise.

Introduce yourself and share with the group:

- Your name
- Where you were born and where you grew up
- What you do for a living, or how you spend your day-to-day life
- A little about your family (are you married, do you have children, siblings, etc.)
- What interested you in this study

In the last few years, what event has caused you the most concern? Why?

SHARE TOGETHER

Have each member of your group share a prayer request, if they have one. Write down each person's request and commit to praying for one another throughout the week.

CLOSE IN PRAYER

Stay Calm

OPEN IN PRAYER

DISCUSS TOGETHER

ICEBREAKER QUESTION: What do you believe happens to people when they die? Have you ever heard of someone who had a near-death experience and saw visions of the afterlife? Do you have specific beliefs or expectations of what the afterlife will be like?

QUESTION 1: God's desire is that our hearts would be calm, no matter what is happening in the world around us. As you think of what it means for you to be calm, which of the following words or phrases come to mind?

quiet   sleep   reading a book

running   solitude   in the mountains   good food

fellowship   at the beach   music

silence   family   Scripture

Other:

Read John 14:1; John 13:21

QUESTION 2: Explore the difference between being troubled and having troubles. What is the point at which your troubles become a burden, the point at which your response is sinful?

Read John 13:33, 36

QUESTION 3: Jesus warned the disciples that they would have trouble in this life (and we will too). How did He instruct them to deal with those troubles?

Read John 14:1 again

QUESTION 4: According to this passage, how do we calm our troubled hearts? What role does faith play in providing peace?

QUESTION 5: Dr. Jeremiah asked if you had put your trust in Jesus. Did you raise your hand? Why or why not?

Read John 14:2

QUESTION 6: In the video, Dr. Jeremiah explains that heaven is a real place—not a feeling or a longed-for utopia or just a version of your best self, but a literal place prepared for real people. Does your impression of heaven fit that description in John 14:2? How can your belief in heaven give you confidence in a chaotic world?

Read John 14:3

QUESTION 7: What promise does Jesus ask us to believe? Is this promise difficult for you to trust?

Read John 17:24

QUESTION 8: The Bible tells us that Jesus has gone to prepare a place *for us*. That He has told His Father He desires to spend eternity with us. What does this tell you about the love God has for us? How does that calm your heart and give you confidence?

Read the following story:

There was a man of great wealth who had many homes on this earth; so many homes that he could hardly keep up with them. He would have a difficult time remembering which home he was in. He was very wealthy, but he got cancer. And although they took him to every specialist around the world they could not find a way to keep that cancer from destroying his life. Finally the doctor told him that he was going to die. Hospice was sent to his home. This very wealthy man had a four-year-old little girl, and her mother was trying to help her understand what was going on with her daddy. She didn't understand death. Her mother just told her that daddy was going to go away to another place.

One day this little girl went into her daddy's bedroom, climbed upon the bed and said, "Papa, can I ask you something?" He said, "Sweetie, what do you want?" She said, "Papa, do you have a home in that place where you're going?" And this man who had spent all of his life building homes on this earth had never spent any time caring for the home where he was going to spend eternity.

Read John 14:4–6; Proverbs 14:2

QUESTION 9: In the video, Dr. Jeremiah told us four things that Jesus wants us to believe in: a person, a place, a promise, and a plan. Many of us think we can get to heaven on our own, but Jesus promises that He is the only way. If you take a birds-eye view of your life, does it show evidence that you are following Jesus' plan or your own?

SHARE TOGETHER

Have each member of your group share a prayer request. Write down each person's request and commit to praying for one another throughout the week.

CLOSE IN PRAYER

Stay Compassionate

OPEN IN PRAYER

DISCUSS TOGETHER

ICEBREAKER QUESTION: Some people have joked that they will lock all the doors and pull up the drawbridge in these difficult times we're facing! What's your strategy for getting through tough economic, political, or social times?

Read 1 Thessalonians 2:18

QUESTION 1: Have you ever tried to do something for God that Satan has hindered? Describe the situation. What is an appropriate response to Satan thwarting your efforts?

QUESTION 2: In the video, Dr. Jeremiah asked what kind of prayer you would pray if you were Paul and you knew the stress under which the Thessalonians were living. What is your response?

Read 1 Thessalonians 3:12; Psalm 116:5; Lamentations 3:22, 23

QUESTION 3: We don't always feel motivated toward compassion, especially when we're suffering ourselves. Why do Christians have a unique position to extend compassion to others?

QUESTION 4: Dr. Jeremiah pointed out in 1 Thessalonians 3:12 that we must love everyone, even people we don't like. What is the key to doing this? Who are the "to all"s in your life—who is it most difficult for you to love? Why?

Read 1 Thessalonians 4:9, 10

QUESTION 5: The Thessalonians had plenty of love in their hearts; Paul confirmed this. What they needed was love-in-action. They needed to express the love God had put in their hearts. Have you seen this same phenomenon in our culture today? In what way are Christians quick to feel compassion but slow to act on it?

QUESTION 6: Do you believe there should be any prerequisite for Christian ministry? (For example, in order to receive acts of service or compassion, a person must listen to a sermon.)

Read John 13:35

QUESTION 7: If a stranger watched you for one day, would they know you are a Christian? Why or why not?

QUESTION 8: Dr. Jeremiah noted the five ways Paul demonstrated his love-in-action from 1 Thessalonians 3:12. Match those ways in the following verses. How can you apply these actions to situations in your own life?

1 Thess. 1:2	he was kind, gentle and considerate toward them
1 Thess. 1:6	he thanked God for them and prayed for them
1 Thess. 2:2	he preached the gospel to them
1 Thess 2:7, 8	he sacrificed for them
1 Thess 2:9	he suffered for them

Read 1 Thessalonians 3:13

QUESTION 9: What is the purpose of compassion?

SHARE TOGETHER

Give everyone an opportunity to share prayer requests, and commit to pray for them throughout the week.

CLOSE IN PRAYER

Stay Constructive

OPEN IN PRAYER

DISCUSS TOGETHER

ICEBREAKER QUESTION: In the video, Dr. Jeremiah gave the example of the atheistic bus ads. Have you ever encountered aggressive in-your-face atheism? What was the situation, and how did you respond? If you haven't experienced it personally, describe an atheistic influence you see dominating culture or media today.

QUESTION 1: In what ways has our generation torn down, rather than built up, our society?

Read 2 Timothy 3:1–5

QUESTION 2: Paul warns us that difficult times are ahead of us. We shouldn't get too comfortable with our lives here on earth, because they could change at any time. Briefly write an example you've seen in your life of each of the characteristics of people that Paul warns us about in the last days.

Self-absorbed

Money-hungry

Self-promoting

Stuck-up

Profane

Contemptuous of parents

Crude

Coarse

Dog-eat-dog

Unbending

Slanderers

Impulsively wild

Savage

Cynical

Treacherous

Ruthless

Bloated windbags

Addicted to lust

Allergic to God

Making a show of religion

QUESTION 3: What does Paul instruct us to do regarding these people?

Read Luke 5:8, 10

QUESTION 4: Jesus' call to Peter was a time of tearing down for him (as he realized his sinfulness) and of building him up (as Jesus promised him he'd be a fisher of men). How has Jesus' call on your life resulted in a tearing down and building up of sorts? What will you do with that reconstruction in your life?

Read John 21:15–17

QUESTION 5: Dr. Jeremiah explained that Jesus used the word *agape* for "love" in his first two questions, but Peter responded with the word for "fond." What is the significance of these words for love used in this section? Do you identify with Peter in this scene?

QUESTION 6: How does this scene with Peter connect to the idea that we, as Christians, must be in the business of being constructive within the church?

Read 1 Corinthians 10:23, 24

QUESTION 7: How does having a focus on construction (or, building up) help us to be more others focused?

QUESTION 8: Many Christians search for a church asking the question, "Does this church meet my needs?" But what is an appropriate attitude for Christian community?

Read Romans 14:19

QUESTION 9: Does edification require active participation on our part, or can we simply avoid tearing others down? Why is it harder sometimes to build up than to tear down?

SHARE TOGETHER

Have each member of your group share a prayer request. Write down each person's request and commit to praying for one another throughout the week.

CLOSE IN PRAYER

Stay Challenged

OPEN IN PRAYER

DISCUSS TOGETHER

Read the following story:

For all of his 76 years, Romanian-born Liviu Librescu met life's challenges head-on. As a child in Romania during World War II he had been confined to a Jewish ghetto while his father was sentenced to a forced labor camp. But Liviu survived the Holocaust, and he determined to fulfill his dream of becoming an engineer. And in spite of the Communist Party ruling Romania during all of that time, he did indeed get his degree.

He completed an undergraduate engineering degree and then a Ph.D. at the Institute of Fluid Mechanics at Romania's Academy of Science. As a brilliant professor he was widely esteemed—within Romania. But Communist rule would not allow him to publish his research outside of Romania. So, at great risk, he smuggled his papers out of Romania to publishers in other countries.

After three years of overcoming obstacles, Dr. Librescu and his wife were granted permission to emigrate to Israel in 1978. And there he taught at the Tel-Aviv University for seven years and finally accepted a one-year position as a visiting professor at Virginia Tech University in Blacksburg, Virginia.

In 1985, his family moved there, and they became part of the university family. He became one of Virginia Tech's most popular and respected professors and researchers.

Throughout his career, Dr. Librescu compiled a list of awards and recognitions that are too long for me to even mention, but they were evidence of how the man lived his life—with strenuous and lavish commitment and generosity to all of the opportunities that he received. He led his family to live that way, and everyone who knew him saw a man who was living his life wide open. For all of his 76 years, he exemplified in his life the kind of diligence that reflects the image of God in human beings.

When the professor himself was asked in 2005 why he continued to work so hard at such an advanced age, he said, "It is not a question of organizations or calculations. If I had the pleasure to do this, then I will put time aside to do this. It is a matter of my personal freedom. If you are limited, then you miss the freedom. And I would like to be fluid. I would like to be free as a bird and fly everywhere."

Well, that's the way he lived his life—overcoming obstacles for more than seven decades to give everything he had to what he loved. He continued to teach at Virginia Tech well past retirement because life itself was a challenge for him. He never gave himself permission to stop as long as his students needed him. In fact, it was his diligence that cost him his life and served as the ultimate illustration of what it means to live with no reservations.

On April 16, 2007, when a heavily-armed, deranged student entered the classroom buildings on the Virginia Tech campus and began randomly killing and wounding students and staff, Dr. Librescu was teaching a class of around 20 students. As soon as it became obvious that the shooter might target his classroom, the 76-year-old professor immediately threw himself against the inside of the classroom door and instructed his students to flee out the windows to safety. One of the last students to exit the classroom remembers seeing the professor leaning against the door and then falling, fatally wounded by bullets that came through the door and ended his life. All 20 of his students, some with broken legs from the two-story fall, survived the incident.

And we have to ask ourselves this question: What would make someone sacrifice himself for the sake of others? For Liviu Librescu, it was the culmination of a life of overcoming challenges and remaining diligent to the end. After the attack, a student summarized the professor's actions. He said, "It's one of those things where every little thing you do can save somebody's life."

I tell this story for a reason. And that reason is really expressed by Dr. Librescu's friend, the department head where he served. He said, "[Professor Librescu] was an extremely tolerant man who mentored scholars from all over our troubled world." The professor was no stranger to trouble, but he wasn't intimidated by it either. From childhood, his commitment to living for others created peace in "our troubled world." Christians live in the same world. And we are called by God to take up our cross and march into the trouble for the sake of Christ—not knowing but that one little thing we might do might save someone's life not only for time but for eternity.

ICEBREAKER QUESTION: What challenges or inspires you? What could you do with passion every day for the rest of your life?

Read 2 Peter 3:14

QUESTION 1: What is the importance of living with diligence in these troubled times?

Read 2 Peter 1:3, 4

QUESTION 2: Have you ever realized that you have *everything* you need—not most things, but everything you need—for life and godliness?

QUESTION 3: Where does Peter tell us we can find the "everything" that we have? How do we get that?

QUESTION 4: In the video, what did Dr. Jeremiah explain is the purpose of diligence?

QUESTION 5: Dr. Jeremiah asked us if we are being diligent to use what God has given us for the purpose of diligence. Circle the areas below in which you feel you're gifted, or add your own. And explain how you use that gift to honor God.

Hospitality	Compassion	Leadership	Loyalty
Academics	Honesty	Sports	Creativity
Logistics	Finances	Relationships	Performance Arts
Patience	Service		
Other:			

Read 1 Peter 1:3–7

QUESTION 6: What are the prerequisites for diligence in your Christian life, according to Peter?

Read 2 Peter 1:8

QUESTION 7: Discuss the ways this verse shows that we have stability, vitality, and reality in our Christian life if we maintain diligence in our faith.

Read the following story:

A little boy fell out of bed during the night, and told his mother, "I went to sleep too close to where I got in." That's what happens to too many of the children of God. They remain children by dozing off at the very entry point of their faith.

QUESTION 8: In what way are you failing to be diligent, falling asleep too close to the edge in your spiritual life?

SHARE TOGETHER

Have each member of your group share a prayer request. Write down each person's request and commit to praying for one another throughout the week.

CLOSE IN PRAYER

Stay Connected

OPEN IN PRAYER

DISCUSS TOGETHER

ICEBREAKER QUESTION: When you find yourself in a crisis or simply feeling down, who is the one person (living or dead) you wish were there to comfort you?

Read Malachi 3:16

QUESTION 1: What happens when God's people speak to one another in community? What does that tell us about how much God values community?

Read Hebrews 10:22–25

QUESTION 2: In the video, Dr. Jeremiah said he underlined three words in this passage. Fill in the blanks below:

1. Let us draw near with a true heart in full assurance of _____.

2. Let us hold fast the confession of our _____.

3. Let us consider one another in order to stir up _____ and good works.

What instructions are given on how to make sure these exhortations are followed?

Read Acts 2:46a; Hebrews 10:25; 2 Thessalonians 2:1

QUESTION 3: The average churchgoing person in California attends Sunday services 3 out of 5 Sundays. How often do you attend church? What are valid excuses to you for not attending (for example: a sick child, an early tee time, etc.)?

QUESTION 4: Think about people who don't have the opportunity to go to church (people in rest homes, hospitals, etc.). What can you do to take church to them? In what ways would it be similar to your church experience, and how would it be different?

Read Acts 2:46b; Acts 20:20

QUESTION 5: How did the early church gather for small-group fellowship?

Read Hebrews 10:24; John 13:34; Hebrews 3:13; James 5:15; Galatians 6:2

QUESTION 6: What is the benefit of meeting together for fellowship? Is it a burden we must bear, or a joy we are privileged to share in? Share an example of the power of community from your own life.

Read 1 Corinthians 13:13; Hebrews 10:22–24

QUESTION 7: What three things does a person receive when they gather together in real Christian fellowship? How does fellowship with other believers impact your personal relationship with Christ?

Read the following story:

> There's a legend about a church in southern Europe called the "House of Many Lamps." It was built in the sixteenth century, and had no provision for artificial light except for a receptacle at every seat for the placement of a lamp. In the evenings, as the people came to church, they would carry their own light with them. When they entered the church building, they would place their lamp in the receptacle as they began to worship. If someone stayed away, his place remained dark. If more than a few stayed away, the darkness seemed to spread. It took the regular presence of every member to illuminate that sanctuary.

QUESTION 8: How does fellowship prepare you for the chaotic times we live in?

SHARE TOGETHER

Have each member of your group share a prayer request, as we all have unmet needs and desires in our heart. Commit to pray for each other throughout the week.

CLOSE IN PRAYER

Stay Centered

OPEN IN PRAYER

DISCUSS TOGETHER

ICEBREAKER QUESTION: Most of us long for some sense of security in this life, although others love risk and can't wait to take the next daring missions trip. Which describes you better—a person who loves the comfort of the daily rhythm of life, or a person who thrives on dare-devil challenges?

Read Philippians 3:20

QUESTION 1: How do you set your heart and mind on the things of heaven?

Read Colossians 3:2; Psalm 62:10b

QUESTION 2: How do these two verses connect to give us a proper view of how we should focus our life on earth? Are we to ignore earthly things, acting as if we're citizens of heaven only? Or is it okay to direct energy toward the pursuits of this life?

Read the following story:

> Think for a moment, about a compass that you might carry on a hike. You can turn your feet in any direction, but the arrow of the compass will faithfully point to magnetic north. That way, should you ever become lost, the compass will align your position for you. In life, our true north is Christ. Whatever direction our world's path may twist, however off-path it may wander, our lives should point faithfully to the one and only Lord of every place, every time, every situation. When He is our determining point, everything will find its proper orientation.

Read Colossians 3:1

QUESTION 3: How do you base your identity in Christ?

Read Colossians 3:1; 1 Corinthians 15:22; Galatians 2:20; Romans 6:4; Ephesians 2:6

QUESTION 4: Circle the ways in which these verses tell us we share in Christ's death. How does this give you confidence in Him?

We're raised with Him.

We'll be mocked as He was.

Our family will leave us.

We'll be made alive with Him.

We're crucified with Him.

We're buried with Him.

We will have dominion in heaven.

We're seated with Christ.

QUESTION 5: How does sharing in Christ's death help us to set our affection on Him?

Read 2 Timothy 2:13; Hebrews 3:18

QUESTION 6: How do we know we can trust Christ more than anything else in this life?

Read Matthew 6:33; Luke 10:38–42; Matthew 6:19, 20

QUESTION 7: How do we stay centered on Christ?

Question 8: Dr. Jeremiah explained that when he had cancer, his priorities were reordered. Have your priorities shifted lately? Why or why not?

Question 9: In the video, Dr. Jeremiah confessed to being a "Martha"—wanting to act immediately in times of crisis. Do you see traits of Martha in your own life? What does it look like to be a "Mary"?

SHARE TOGETHER

If anyone in your group has a prayer request, share them and commit to pray for them over the next week. Read Isaiah 26:3 aloud, and close in prayer.

CLOSE IN PRAYER

Stay Confident

OPEN IN PRAYER

DISCUSS TOGETHER

ICEBREAKER QUESTION: Describe a time when you've witnessed something happen around you that you felt you must involve yourself in. It could be something specific, such as reporting a drunk driver, or something global, such as organizing a conference to educate others on the AIDS pandemic. Why did you feel compelled to get involved in this situation?

Read 2 Timothy 4:1, 2; Amos 8:11

QUESTION 1: What do the people of God need when they face chaotic times?

QUESTION 2: What do you rely on in your life—what or whom do you expect to be there for you always? What does Scripture say is the only thing we can be sure of?

QUESTION 3: In the video, Dr. Jeremiah said that we need a serious word from God. Why must we take God's Word seriously?

QUESTION 4: Paul talks about being convinced of the gospel, which can be interpreted as "presenting a strong appeal" or defending the gospel as an attorney would. Why is it important that we consider the evidence of the gospel as opposed to simply taking it on faith?

Read Titus 1:9; Colossians 1:28

QUESTION 5: Dr. Jeremiah quoted Amy Carmichael saying, "If you've never been hurt by a word from God, it's probable you've never heard God speak." In what ways has God's Word convicted *your* spirit? Describe a time when you've felt the power of Scripture to speak truth into your life in the form of a rebuke or conviction.

QUESTION 6: The Bible should convince our minds and convict our spirits, but it should also comfort our souls. Why is it necessary for our souls to find comfort in Scripture? In what way does that help us find balance in a chaotic world?

Read 2 Timothy 4:2; Acts 20:19, 20

QUESTION 7: How should a Christian relate to someone who is caught up in the chaos of earthly living?

Read the following story:

> Corrie ten Boom, survivor of the Nazi concentration camps in World War II, once managed to get a Bible and to read it to fellow prisoners. "The blacker the night around us grew," she recalled, "the brighter and truer and more beautiful burned the Word of God." And indeed the nighttime of her life grew black. She endured the deaths of her father and her beloved sister Betsie. She survived humiliation, cruelty, and neglect. But the Word of God, and the peace of God flowing from it, brought her through the long nightmare so that she might emerge to bless the world with her message of hope.

QUESTION 8: How is your life getting "blacker" and in what ways does the Word of God burn beautifully?

Read Psalm 119:165

QUESTION 9: How will we find peace, according to the psalmist? Are you willing to make the commitment it will take for you to find peace in the midst of *any* struggle?

SHARE TOGETHER

Share your prayer requests as a group, and commit to pray for one another throughout the week. Consider committing to reading the Bible for a set amount of time each day this week.

CLOSE IN PRAYER

Stay Consistent

OPEN IN PRAYER

DISCUSS TOGETHER

ICEBREAKER QUESTION: Do you have any daily habits that you almost never break (for example, you have Cheerios with blueberries every single morning for breakfast)? Or are you the type of person who never does the same thing twice?

Read 1 John 2:28a

QUESTION 1: What is the significance of John's calling his readers "little children"?

Read 1 John 2:6

QUESTION 2: According to the video, what does the word *abide* mean? Brainstorm practical ways you can "abide in Christ" on a daily basis.

QUESTION 3: How does a person become consistently Christlike? What does Dr. Jeremiah explain is the way to learn that?

Read 1 John 2:6, 10, 14, 17

QUESTION 4: Read the above verses and match the ways God's Word in us makes us more consistent.

1 John 2:6   consistently confident

1 John 2:10   consistently compliant (consistently consistent forever)

1 John 2:14   consistently caring

1 John 2:17   consistently Christlike

Read John 4:34

QUESTION 5: We've studied that our example to follow in trying to live with confidence in chaotic times is the life of Jesus. But how did Jesus make His decisions? Whose will did He conform to? Does knowing this make an impact on your daily struggle to live a holy life?

Read 1 John 2:28

QUESTION 6: What should be the motive for our consistency in our walk with Christ? Why?

Read 2 Corinthians 5:10

QUESTION 7: What is the "judgment seat of Christ"? Knowing that one day we'll face that judgment seat, how should we adjust our walk with Christ today? Be specific.

Read the following story:

Charles Swindoll has a wonderful story in one of his books that I've always loved. He worked in a factory when he was a student at seminary. And every day when the whistle blew at five o'clock, everybody would hustle around and get their lunch pails and their clothes and you know fifteen minutes or so after five they'd leave. But there was a guy who worked in there who seemed uncannily able, when the whistle blew at five o'clock, within just a second or so he had his lunch pail in his hand, his coat over his shoulder and he was walking out the door. One day, Swindoll said, "How do you do it?" and he adds, "I'll never forget what he said: 'Let me tell you something, Sonny. I just stay ready to keep from gittin' ready." [1]

---

1   Based on Charles Swindoll, *The Tale of the Tardy Oxcart*. Nashville, TN: Word Publishing, Inc, 1998, 464–465.

QUESTION 8: In the video, Dr. Jeremiah talked about the importance of reps. What is one specific habit you're going to develop to aid in the consistency of your walk with Jesus?

SHARE TOGETHER

Have each member of your group share a prayer request and/or a new habit they want to commit to implementing in their walk. Write down each person's request and commit to praying for one another through the week.

CLOSE IN PRAYER

Stay Committed

OPEN IN PRAYER

DISCUSS TOGETHER

Icebreaker Question: What are the pet-peeves in your life that drive you to impatience? Is it heavy traffic, whining children, a messy house, a phone ringing off the hook? When do you lose your patience?

Read James 5:7

QUESTION 1: Why are we to be patient as we wait for the coming of the Lord? What do you think impatience in waiting on God looks like?

QUESTION 2: In the video, Dr. Jeremiah said that it is often through the difficult seasons of our lives that God does His most profound work in us. When have you seen this to be true in your own life? What did you learn about God, yourself, your culture, your community? In what ways was it difficult, and in what ways did you find comfort in the process?

Read James 5

QUESTION 3: Read this chapter aloud and record how many times the word *patience* is mentioned. How is patience connected to our faith?

QUESTION 4: Dr. Jeremiah explained that the people James was writing to were facing difficult times, feeling as if the only way to get any relief was through Christ's return. Has the current chaos in our economy and in world politics caused you to long for Christ's return? Have you ever found yourself pleading, "Come, Lord Jesus, come"?

Read James 5:7

QUESTION 5: How does this illustration of waiting for the rains apply to *your* life and faith today? How is your existence dependent upon your patient faith?

Read 2 Peter 3:3, 4

QUESTION 6: Have you heard anyone speak this way about our time now? Can you think of a person or media outlet who continually mocks the return of Christ? Explain.

Read James 5:8

QUESTION 7: What is the implication of patience Dr. Jeremiah draws here? What must we do while we wait patiently for Christ's return? How do we do this in our daily lives?

Read Titus 2:13; 1 Corinthians 1:7; Colossians 3:2; 1 Thessalonians 1:10

QUESTION 8: Read these verses and make a note of what they say about waiting. How does knowing we must wait on Christ give us confidence?

QUESTION 9: Do you feel confident that you can handle the things the world throws at you with God's grace and faith in Him?

SHARE TOGETHER

Share prayer requests, and commit to pray for each other throughout the week.

CLOSE IN PRAYER

Stay Convinced

OPEN IN PRAYER

DISCUSS TOGETHER

Icebreaker Question: Have you ever waited with great anticipation for something in your life? Describe the event and your feelings about it.

Read Romans 13:11; 2 Timothy 4:2; 1 Thessalonians 3

QUESTION 1: As you read back over some of the thematic verses we've studied so far, what is similar about each prophecy for final days?

Read Romans 13:11, 12 again.

QUESTION 2: Write down all the time references you read in these two verses. What is the significance of so much emphasis on time?

QUESTION 3: In the video, Dr. Jeremiah read the following definition of *sleep* according to the *Encyclopedia Britannica*: "a state of inactivity, with a loss of consciousness, and a decrease in responsiveness to events taking place." Paul commands that we wake from our sleep in Romans 13:11. What does that look like in the life of a believer? Be specific.

Read Exodus 20:12–17; Romans 13:8–10

QUESTION 4: Why does Paul draw the connection between the Law (the Ten Commandments) and Christ's return? How do they influence one another?

Read Romans 13:12

QUESTION 5: What are we to "cast off"? Examine your life. What specific things do you need to abandon in order to move forward in your relationship with God? Come up with a plan for how you will do that.

Read Romans 13:13

QUESTION 6: As you read through this list of sins, look up each word in the dictionary and write out the definition you find there. Just as Paul warns us to wake from our sleep, don't let your mind gloss over these sins. Where do you see them taking root in your life? And how are they undermining your confidence in our chaotic world?

Orgies—

Drunkenness—

Sexual immorality—

Sensuality—

Quarrelling—

Jealousy—

Read Romans 13:14

QUESTION 7: In the video, Dr. Jeremiah told the story of the man and the doughnuts. Can you think of a time you made provision for the flesh? How can you do things in the future to change that? Be specific.

QUESTION 8: Can you think of any images or experiences that have illustrated to you God's love poured out on us? How does the understanding of that power convince you that Christ will return?

SHARE TOGETHER

Spend time in worship as a group, praying about the glory of Christ's return. Share prayer requests and commit to honor each other in prayer throughout the week.

CLOSE IN PRAYER

PRAYER REQUESTS

PRAYER REQUESTS

PRAYER REQUESTS

THREE
GREAT WAYS
TO FURTHER
YOUR STUDY

FROM THE *NEW YORK TIMES* BEST-SELLING AUTHOR OF
WHAT IN THE WORLD IS GOING ON?

DR. DAVID JEREMIAH

LIVING WITH
CONFIDENCE
IN A CHAOTIC
WORLD

**WHAT
ON EARTH
SHOULD WE
DO NOW?**

INCORPORATE THESE CORRELATING
STUDY MATERIALS
BY AUTHOR DR. DAVID JEREMIAH

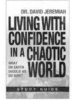

STUDY GUIDE

This 128-page study guide correlates with the *Living with Confidence in a Chaotic World* messages by Dr. David Jeremiah. Each lesson provides an outline, overview, and application study questions for each chapter.

AUDIO MESSAGE ALBUM
10 AUDIO MESSAGES

The material found in this book originated from messages preached by Dr. David Jeremiah at Shadow Mountain Community Church where he serves as Senior Pastor. These ten messages are conveniently packaged in one audio album.

DVD MESSAGE PRESENTATIONS
10 DVD MESSAGES

Watch Dr. Jeremiah deliver the ten *Living with Confidence in a Chaotic World* original messages in the special DVD collection.

SMALL GROUP STUDY CURRICULUM

The *Living with Confidence in a Chaotic World* DVD-Based Small Group Kit will take your small group or Sunday school class through ten weeks of Dr. Jeremiah's teaching for living with certain hope in our uncertain times.

THE NEW YORK TIMES BEST SELLER
THAT STARTED IT ALL!

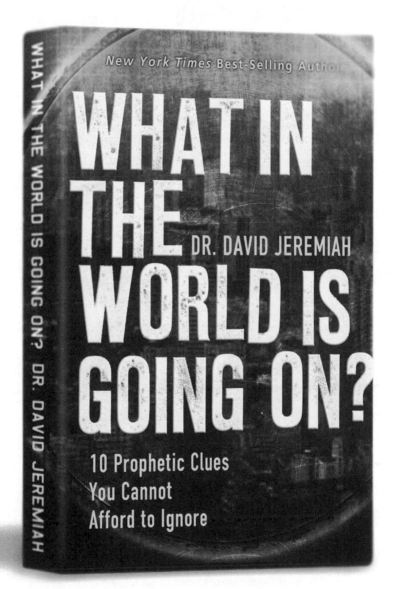

The Bible prophecy prequel to
Living with Confidence in a Chaotic World
by Dr. David Jeremiah

IS THE TURBULENT ECONOMIC & POLITICAL STATE OF THIS WORLD ACTUALLY PROPHESIED IN THE BIBLE?

If so, what are we to do about it? It is hard to piece together all this information in a way that gives a comprehensive picture of what the End Times will look like. That's why so many theories abound. And that's why Dr. David Jeremiah has written *What in the World Is Going On?*, a unique book that cuts through the hundreds of books and numerous theories to identify the ten essential biblical prophecies that are affecting our world today.

There is no other book like this. You'll find it is the ultimate study tool for understanding the future. You'll have a greater sense of comfort that, even in these turbulent times, God is indeed in control. If Bible prophecy has always been a mystery to you, Dr. Jeremiah's book will help you solve the mystery. At last, Bible prophecy can make sense, and make a difference. It's never been more important. *What in the World Is Going On?* is shocking and eye-opening but essential reading in these turbulent days.

WHAT IN THE WORLD IS GOING ON? BRINGS BIBLE PROPHECY TO LIGHT ON:
- The oil crisis
- The resurgence of Russia
- The new axis of evil
- The importance of Israel
- The new powers of the European Union

WHAT IN THE WORLD IS GOING ON?

is available in fine bookstores everywhere and through Turning Point where you will also find a correlating study guide, ten message CD album, DVD presentations, and small group curriculum of this book.

VISIT DAVIDJEREMIAH.ORG TO ORDER

OTHER TITLES
BY DR. DAVID JEREMIAH

CAPTURED BY GRACE `A NEW YORK TIMES BEST-SELLER!`

By following the dramatic story of the "Amazing Grace" hymnwriter, John Newton, and the apostle Paul's own encounter with the God of grace, David Jeremiah helps readers understand the liberating power of permanent forgiveness and mercy.

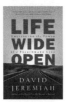

LIFE WIDE OPEN

In this energizing book, Dr. David Jeremiah opens our eyes to how we can live a life that exudes an attitude of hope and enthusiasm . . . a life of passion . . . a LIFE WIDE OPEN! *Life Wide Open* offers a vision, both spiritual and practical, of what our life can be when we allow the power of passion to permeate our souls.

SIGNS OF LIFE `A NEW YORK TIMES BEST-SELLER!`

How does the world recognize us as God's ambassadors? In *Signs of Life* you will take a journey that will lead you to a fuller understanding of the marks that identify you as a Christian, signs that will advertise your faith and impact souls for eternity.

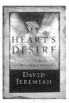

MY HEART'S DESIRE

How would you answer a pollster who appeared at your church asking for a definition of worship? Is it really a sin to worship without sacrifice? When you finish studying *My Heart's Desire*, you'll have not just an answer, but the biblical answer to that all-important question.

SEARCHING FOR HEAVEN ON EARTH

Join Dr. Jeremiah as he traces Solomon's path through the futility of:

- The search for wisdom and knowledge
- Wild living and the pursuit of pleasure
- Burying oneself in work
- Acquiring as much wealth as possible

Dr. Jeremiah takes readers on a discovery to find out what really matters in life, the secret to enjoying "heaven on earth."

WHEN YOUR WORLD FALLS APART

When Your World Falls Apart recounts Dr. Jeremiah's battle against cancer and the real-life stories of others who have struggled with tragedy. Highlighting ten Psalms of encouragement, each chapter is a beacon of light in those moments when life seems hopeless.

SLAYING THE GIANTS

Loneliness. Discouragement. Worry. Anger. Procrastination. Doubt. Fear. Guilt. Temptation. Resentment. Failure. Jealousy. Have these giants infiltrated your life? Do you need the tools to slay these daunting foes? With practical appeal and personal warmth, Dr. Jeremiah's book, *Slaying the Giants in Your Life* will become your very own giant-slaying manual.

TURNING POINTS & SANCTUARY

These 365-day devotionals by Dr. Jeremiah will equip you to live with God's perspective. These topically arranged devotionals enable you to relate biblical truths to the reality of everyday living—every day of the year. Perfect for yourself or your next gift-giving occasion, *Turning Points* and *Sanctuary* are beautifully packaged with a padded cover, original artwork throughout, and a ribbon page marker.

**THESE RESOURCES FROM DR. DAVID JEREMIAH CAN
BE ORDERED AT WWW.DAVIDJEREMIAH.ORG**

STAY CONNECTED
TO THE TEACHING OF DR. DAVID JEREMIAH

Take advantage of two great ways to let Dr. David Jeremiah give you
spiritual direction everyday! Both are absolutely FREE!

TURNING POINTS MAGAZINE AND DEVOTIONAL

Receive Dr. David Jeremiah's monthly
magazine, *Turning Points* each month:

- Monthly Study Focus
- 48 pages of life-changing reading
- Relevant Articles
- Special Features
- Humor Section
- Family Section
- Daily devotional readings for each
  day of the month
- Bible study resource offers
- Live Event Schedule
- Radio & Television Information

YOUR DAILY TURNING POINT E-DEVOTIONAL

Start your day off right! Find words of inspiration
and spiritual motivation waiting for you on your
computer every morning! You can receive a daily
e-devotion communication from David Jeremiah
that will strengthen your walk with God and
encourage you to live the authentic Christian life.

Sign up for these two **free** services by visiting
us online at www.DavidJeremiah.org and clicking
on MAGAZINE to sign up for your monthly copy
of *Turning Points* and your Daily Turning Point.

⬆ MAXIMUM CHURCH

READY! SET! GROWTH!

LET DR. JEREMIAH'S MAXIMUM CHURCH TAKE YOUR CHURCH THERE.

With a united vision to strengthen the Body of Christ and reach the community, your church can experience spiritual and fiscal growth through creative and compelling campaigns.

With over forty years of ministry experience, founder Dr. David Jeremiah now shares his passion for pulpit teaching and church leadership by offering solid Bible teaching campaigns designed to stimulate the spiritual and fiscal growth of local churches. Maximum Church campaigns are created for full-spectrum ministry including preaching, teaching, drama, small group Bible curriculum, and suggested Sunday school material—all supported by electronic, print, and audio visual files.

SIGNS OF LIFE

Lead your church to become one of Christ-like influence in your community as you take the five Life Signs discussed in this book and apply them to the lives of your congregation.

This campaign is based on Dr. David Jeremiah's best-selling book *Signs of Life*.

CAPTURED BY GRACE

Based on the best-selling book *Captured by Grace* by David Jeremiah, this ministry growth campaign will help your church and community discover the depths of God's unrelenting love and grace.

For more information on Maximum Church,
VISIT WWW.MAXIMUMCHURCH.COM